CONTENT

Introduction 4

Vegetable Lasagna 5

Vegetable Indian Dal Soup 7

Black Bean and Sweet Potatoes 9

Sambar 11

Soup with Sweet Potatoes 13

Mushroom Paste 14

„Risotto" 15

Stuffed Peppers 17

Creamy Pumpkin Tamta 18

Vegetable Paella 19

Quesadillas 21

Blueberry Cupcakes 22

Quinoa Salad 23

Vegetable Thai Peanut 24

Palak Paneer 26

Baked Tortilla Chips 28

Tamantas Salad 30

Boras Sauce and Pasta 31

Halwa Pudding of Semolina 32

Carrot Halwa 33

Gazpacho 34

Coconut Barfi 35

Pistachio Barfi 36

Lintel Soup with Vegetables 38

Pie with Raisins and Spices 39

Fresh Young Corn Salad 40

Pears in Red Wine 41

Spinach and Yogurt Raita Salad 43

Cucumber and Yogurt Raita Salad 44

Saffron Rice Pudding 45

Paneer Sabji 46

Tahini – A Raw Food Recipe 48

Strawberry Soup 49

Black Bean Soup 50

Baked Parmesan Zucchini 51

Baked Parmesan Mushrooms 52

Roasted Potatoes 1 53

Baked Green Bean 54

Honey Glazed Carrots 55

Roasted Mushrooms 56

Easy Creamed Corn 57

Healthy Salad 58

Garlic Roasted Broccoli 59

Baked Asparagus with Sauce 60

Roasted Potatoes 2 61

Introduction

This is the 2nd enlarged edition. The book contains a variety of recipes for Vegetarian Dishes representing national cuisine of various countries. Some of them are easy to make and some are not but it is always nice to cook something new, isn't it?

Thanks to this book you will be able to cook your own "home-style" and surprisingly delicious dishes. Recipes in this book are excellent for festive parties and for typical home lunches and dinners.

The book provides 45 recipes and I hope these recipes will help you diversify your "cooking" life starting from today! Treat yourself, your friends and beloved ones!

Vegetable Lasagna

This lasagna recipe is packed with bell pepper, zucchini and carrots, and tender on the edges.

Ingredients

- 2 tablespoons olive oil
- 4 to 5 ounces baby spinach
- 1 medium zucchini, chopped
- 1 yellow onion, chopped
- Salt, to taste
- 3 carrots, chopped
- 1 red pepper, chopped
- 1 medium red onion, chopped
- 1 teaspoon of turmeric

Sauce (2 cups prepared marinara sauce)

- ¼ cup roughly chopped fresh basil
- 2 tablespoons extra-virgin olive oil
- 1 large can diced tomatoes
- Salt, to taste
- 2 cloves garlic, pressed
- ¼ teaspoon red pepper flakes

- 1 tablespoon of lemon juice

Remaining ingredients

- 2 cups low-fat cottage cheese, divided
- Salt, to taste
- Freshly ground black pepper, to taste
- 9 no-boil lasagna noodles, preferably whole wheat
- 2 cups freshly grated low-moisture, part-skim mozzarella cheese

Cooking

- Preheat the oven to 220 C. To prepare the veggies. In a large skillet over medium heat, warm the olive oil over medium heat. Add the carrots, pepper, zucchini, yellow onion, red onion, salt and 1 teaspoon of turmeric. Cook about 10 minutes.
- Add a few handfuls of spinach. Cook until the spinach has wilted. Repeat with remaining spinach and cook until all the spinach has wilted, about 5 minutes.
- Prepare the tomato sauce: Pour the tomatoes into a mesh sieve and drain off the excess juice for a minute. Put the drained tomatoes into the bowl of a food processor. Add the basil, olive oil, garlic, salt, and red pepper and 1 tablespoon of lemon juice. Pulse the mixture about 10 times, you should have a little over 2 cups sauce.
- Then, pour half of the cottage cheese (1 cup) into the processor and blend it until smooth, about 1 minute.
- Transfer the cooked veggies and spinach mixture to the bowl of the food processor. Pulse until they are more finely chopped, about 6 times. Add the mixture to the bowl of whipped cottage cheese. Top with the remaining cottage cheese, then add ½ teaspoon salt and lots of black pepper. Stir to combine.
- Spread ½ cup tomato sauce evenly over the bottom of a baking dish. Layer 3 lasagna noodles on top. Spread half of the cottage cheese mixture evenly over the noodles. Top with ¾ cup tomato sauce, then sprinkle ½ cup shredded cheese on top.
- Top with 3 more noodles, followed by the remaining cottage cheese mixture. Sprinkle ½ cup shredded cheese. Top with 3 more noodles, then spread ¾ cup tomato sauce over the top to evenly cover the noodles. Sprinkle evenly with 1 cup shredded cheese.
- Bake, covered, for 20 minutes, then remove the cover, rotate the pan by 180 C and continue cooking for about 10 minutes, until the top is turning spotty brown. Remove from oven and let the lasagna cool for 15 to 20 minutes, then slice and serve.

Vegetable Indian Dal Soup

A tasty soup recipe – indispensable source of proteins and other healthy vitamins and microelements.

Ingredients

4 servings:

- 200 g peas
- 2 l water
- 2 teaspoons ground coriander
- 1 teaspoon turmeric (if available)
- 300 g peeled and diced vegetables (carrots, cauliflower or common cabbage, runner beans)
- 1 tablespoon cooking butter
- 2 teaspoons cumin seeds
- ½ dried hot red pepper pod, chopped into pieces
- 3 - 4 tomatoes, washed and cut into 8 wedges each
- 3 teaspoons of salt
- 1 tablespoon chopped green parsley or coriander leaves

Cooking

- Sort out and rinse peas, drain water. Pour 2 l of water in a pot, add peas, ground coriander, turmeric and put at medium heat. Once it boils, skim off the foam and let it boil at medium heat for 30 min, the lid being slightly open, until peas become soft.
- Add vegetables and cook soup for 10 more minutes. In parallel, prepare the seasoning. At medium heat warm up cooking butter in a small pot with handle or in a small dipper. Fry cumin seeds and pepper in hot butter for 30 – 40 sec. Afterwards, add tomatoes, stir and fry for 4 – 5 min. Add seasoning to the soup and season with salt. Stir, remove from heat, close the lid and let the soup stand for a while so that it soaks up with spices flavour. Serve with fresh green parsley or coriander leaves.

Black Bean and Sweet Potatoes

Super black bean and potatoes, smothered in salsa Verde. A delicious, hearty vegetarian recipe.

Ingredients

- 2 small cans diced green chiles
- 2 cloves garlic, pressed
- 2 tablespoons lime juice
- ½ teaspoon ground cumin
- 1,5 pounds sweet potatoes
- 1 ½ cups cooked black beans
- 4 ounces grated cheese, to taste
- ½ cup crumbled feta cheese
- ½ teaspoon chili powder
- Salt, to taste
- Freshly ground black pepper
- ½ cup salsa

Remaining Ingredients

- 1 tablespoon water
- 2 cups mild salsa
- 10 corn tortillas
- 1 cup grated cheese

- 2 tablespoons sour cream
- ½ cup chopped red onion
- ½ cup chopped fresh cilantro

Cooking

- Preheat the oven to 200 degrees Celsius. Slice the sweet potatoes in half lengthwise and coat the flat sides lightly with olive oil. Place the sweet potatoes flat-side down on the baking sheet. Bake them until they are tender and cooked through, about 35 to 40 minutes.
- Pour enough salsa into a baking dish. In a medium mixing bowl, combine all the remaining filling ingredients.
- Once the sweet potatoes are cooked through and cool enough to handle, scoop out the insides with a spoon. Discard the potato skins, and mash up the sweet potato a bit.
- Stir the mashed sweet potato into the bowl of filling, and season to taste with additional salt and pepper.
- Warm up your tortillas, one by one in a skillet, or all at once in a microwave, so they don't break when you bend them. Wrap them in a tea towel so they stay warm. Repeat for all of the tortillas.
- Top with the remaining salsa and cheese. Bake 35 minutes, until sauce is bubbling and the cheese is lightly golden.
- Let cool for about 5 minutes. Add some sour cream and serve.

Sambar

Sambar is usually served either as a garnish or as a seasoning for boiled rice or other dishes. It's a liquid sauce with a small content of vegetables.

There is a great variety of sambar cooking recipes depending on the region, locally grown vegetables and people's own taste.

This is a quite digestible dish, thicker than a common Dal. It's usually served with masala, white rice or bread of any kind.

Ingredients

4 servings:

- 6 cups (1.4 l) water
- 3 teaspoons salt
- 250 g Mung Dal or Tur Dal, or green shelled peas or lentils
- 675 g various vegetables: eggplants, carrots, tomatoes, runner beans or pumpkin
- 50 g tamarind
- 3 tablespoons cooking butter or vegetable oil
- 1 teaspoon mustard seeds

- 1 teaspoon ground cumin seeds
- 2 teaspoons ground coriander
- ¼ teaspoon Cayenne pepper or two pods of fresh hot pepper
- 1 teaspoon turmeric
- 4 tablespoons coconut paste

Cooking

- Boil salted water. Sort out, wash, dry Dal and put it in boiling water. Boil in a pot uncovered for 10 min. Skim off the foam, close the lid and boil at medium heat for 15-25 min, often stirring. Dal should become soft but not completely cooked.
- While Dal is being cooked, wash and dice vegetables. Prepare tamarind water.
- Warm up butter in a pot and fry the mustard seeds. When seeds cease to crack, add ground spices, continue frying for a few seconds, then add vegetables (if you use eggplant, then fry it preliminary until it becomes soft). In 10-15 min, after all vegetables get brown, add coconut paste and fry for 2 more minutes.
- By that time, Dal should be ready. Add vegetables and tamarind juice and stir well. Reduce heat and boil uncovered until ready – Dal should become thick and vegetables soft.

Soup with Sweet Potatoes

This soup is perfect for warming up. It's easy and tasty soup.

Ingredients

- 1 pound sweet potatoes
- Salt, to taste
- 2 tablespoons Thai red curry paste
- 2 tablespoons olive oil
- 1 yellow onion, chopped
- 1 red pepper, chopped
- 1 can chickpeas, rinsed and drained
- 3 cups bunch of kale chopped
- 3 cups cooked whole grains
- 4 cups vegetable broth
- 2 cloves garlic, pressed

Cooking

- In soup pot, heat the oil over medium heat. Stir in the onion, sweet potato, pepper band salt. Heat for five minutes, until the onion starts to soften. Add the curry paste and stir until the vegetables are coated and the curry is fragrant.
- Add your grain of choice and the vegetable broth and water, and stir. Bring the mixture to a boil, then reduce the heat to a simmer and cook for 30 minutes.
- Add the chickpeas and kale. Stir to combine, and cook until the kale is cooked to your liking.
- Taste, and season with more salt as needed. To kick up the flavor a notch and balance the sweetness of the sweet potatoes, stir in the optional cayenne pepper.
- Ladle the soup into bowls and serve.

Mushroom Paste

Ingredients

- 1 glass European walnut soaks for 2-4 hours
- 2 glasses champignons (mushrooms)
  1 garlic clove
- ¼ medium-size yellow onion
- 2 tablespoons olive oil
- 2-3 tablespoons soy sauce, to taste
- 2 tablespoons fresh parsley
- 1 teaspoon fresh or dried sage
- ½ teaspoon fresh-ground peppercorn (any combination of black, white or green)

Cooking

- Drain walnuts and rinse. Coarsely chop mushrooms, onion and garlic. Grind all ingredients together in a food processor (mincing machine). About one hour later, the paste will darken but it's not a problem. Serve with crisp breads or pieces of vegetables.

_____
_____
_____
_____
_____
_____
_____

"Risotto"

This risotto is made with steel-cut oats instead of rice! You'll love it!

Ingredients

- 4 cloves garlic, pressed
- 2 tablespoons butter
- Salt, to taste
- 2 tablespoons olive oil

- 1 tablespoon lemon juice
- 6 cups water
- 2 potatoes, chopped
- Parmesan cheese 1 ½ ounces
- 2 packed cups chopped kale, ribs removed
- ½ cup dry white wine
- 1 red onion, chopped
- Black pepper, to taste

Cooking

- In a soup pot, warm the olive oil. Add the onion, butternut, and the salt. Cook, stirring, about 10 minutes. Add the garlic, kale the oats and stirring about 1 minutes, then add the wine and cook for 1 minute.
- Add the water and salt. Raise the heat to high and bring the mixture to a simmer. Once simmering, reduce the heat to medium-low and simmer, about 25 minutes.
- Remove the pot from the heat and stir in the Parmesan, butter, lemon juice and several twists of black pepper. Let the risotto rest for 5 minutes before serving.

Stuffed Peppers

In a raw version of this dish, which I dearly love, it is better to cut peppers lengthwise into two or even three parts. I prepare stuffing of any nuts and seeds, mixing them in a food processor. My favourite combination is sunflower seeds and European walnuts. 5 various colour peppers cut lengthwise and cleaned of seeds.

Ingredients

- 1 glass European walnuts soaked for at least 2 hours
- 1 glass sunflower seeds soaked for at least 2 hours
- 1 carrot
- 1 glass parsley
- Half of onion

- Half of sweet pepper
- 2 tablespoons soy sauce
- 1 tablespoon ground cumin seeds

(*you can add garlic, miso, celery and dried tomatoes*)

Cooking

- Grind all the ingredients except for peppers in a food processor to obtain a paste.
- Stuff the pepper with a heap.
- Practically completely cover with water, add salt to taste and cook for about 40 minutes over medium heat.

Creamy Pumpkin Tamta

This pumpkin tamta recipe is delicious.

Ingredients

- 1 can crushed tomatoes
- 1 can pumpkin purée
- 2 tablespoons extra-virgin olive oil
- 1 yellow onion, chopped
- 2 cloves garlic, pressed
- ½ teaspoon dried oregano
- ¼ teaspoon ground cinnamon
- Salt, to taste
- 2 tablespoons butter
- Freshly ground black pepper

Cooking

- Warm the olive oil in a large skillet over medium heat. Add the onion, pepper and the salt, to taste. Cook, stirring often, until the onions and pepper are very tender, about 8 minutes.
- Add the garlic, oregano, and cinnamon. While stirring, cook about 1 minute. Add the tomatoes and cook for 1 minute. Add the pumpkin purée and stir. Continue simmering for 5 minutes, then remove it from the heat.
- Carefully transfer the mixture to your blender. Add 1 tablespoon butter. Blend until very smooth and creamy.
- For a more tasty sauce, add another tablespoon of butter. Blend to combine. Stir into warm pasta.

Vegetable Paella

This Spanish dish is perfect for serving at dinner parties. This is the best vegetable paella recipe!

Ingredients

- 3 tablespoons olive oil
- 1 yellow onion, chopped
- Salt, to taste
- 6 garlic cloves, pressed
- 2 teaspoons smoked paprika
- 1 can diced tomatoes, drained
- 2 cups brown rice
- 2 cups vegetable broth
- ½ cup dry white wine
- 1 jar marinated artichoke, drained
- 2 red peppers, stemmed
- ½ cup olives, pitted
- Freshly ground black pepper
- 1 ¼ cup chopped fresh parsley
- 1 tablespoon lemon juice
- ½ cup peas

Cooking

- Preheat the oven to 175 degrees Celsius. Heat 2 tablespoons of the oil in your oven Add the onion and a pinch of salt. Cook until the onions are tender and translucent, about 5 minutes.
- Stir in the garlic and paprika and cook until fragrant, about 30 seconds. Stir in the tomatoes and cook until the mixture begins to darken and thicken slightly, about 2 minutes Stir in the rice and cook until the grains are well coated with tomato mixture, about 1 minute. Stir in the chickpeas, broth, wine, saffron (if using) and the salt.
- Increase the heat to medium-high and bake, until the liquid is absorbed and the rice is tender, about 50 minutes.
- Line a large, rimmed baking sheet with parchment paper for easy cleanup. On the baking sheet, combine the artichoke, peppers, chopped olives, 1 tablespoon of the olive oil, the salt, and freshly ground black pepper, to taste. Then spread the contents evenly across the pan.
- Roast the vegetables on the upper rack until the artichokes and peppers are tender and browned around the edges, about 45 minutes. Remove from the oven and let the vegetables cool for a few minutes. Add ¼ cup parsley to the pan and the lemon juice, and toss to combine. Season with salt and pepper, to taste.
- Sprinkle the peas and roasted vegetables over the baked rice, cover, and let the paella sit for 5 minutes.

Quesadillas

Quesadillas are the perfect quick meal. Enjoy this vegetarian quesadilla recipe!

Ingredients

- 1 tablespoon chopped red bell pepper
- 1 tablespoon chopped red onion and green onion
- ¼ cup cooked black beans or pinto beans, rinsed and drained
- 1 whole-grain flour tortilla (about 8" diameter)
- ½ cup freshly grated cheddar cheese
- 1 teaspoon extra-virgin olive oil, for brushing

Cooking

- Heat a medium skillet over medium heat. Warm your tortilla for about 30 seconds. Flip once more, then sprinkle one-half of the tortilla with about half of the cheese. Cover the cheese evenly with the remaining fillings: beans, bell pepper and onion.
- Sprinkle the remaining cheese over the fillings, and fold over the empty side of the tortilla to enclose the fillings.
- Cook until golden and crispy, about 1 to 2 minutes. Brush the top with a light coating of oil, then flip it and cook until the second side is golden and crispy.
- Remove the skillet from the heat and transfer the quesadilla to a cutting board. Help yourself!

Blueberry Cupcakes

In berry season, not only can you enjoy succulent fruits eaten fresh, but I also encourage you to make very tasty desserts.

Ingredients

- 2 bananas (not too ripe)
- 1,5 glass blueberries
- 1 glass European walnuts
- ¾ coconut flakes
- 2-4 dates
- 2 tablespoons melted coconut butter
- ½ vanilla pod or ½ teaspoon vanilla extract

Cooking

- Mince coconut flakes, walnuts, dates and vanilla seeds or extract in a food processor (mincer). As soon as the dough becomes sticky, paste it up in the moulds.
- Mix banana with blueberries in a blender adding coconut oil in the process. Actually, it's possible to make it without it – it will take more time until it becomes a jelly, about 8 hours as a minimum, or you can let it chill in the fridge.
- Pour jelly in the moulds filled with dough – it is advisable to place them on a tray or a plate. Then you can place the tray in the fridge for at least an hour, still better for 3 hours or more.
- Carefully take out the cupcakes of the silicon moulds. Use a fork while eating – the cakes are quite tough, even frozen.

Quinoa Salad

Very, very taste salad!

Ingredients

- 1 medium bell pepper, chopped
- 1 red onion, chopped
- 1 tablespoon red wine vinegar
- 1 large bunch parsley, chopped
- ¼ cup olive oil

- 1 cup uncooked quinoa
- 2 cups water
- ¼ cup lemon juice
- 2 cloves garlic, pressed
- 1 medium cucumber, chopped
- Salt, to taste
- Freshly ground black pepper, to taste

Cooking

- Mix the rinsed quinoa and the water in a medium saucepan. Cook until the quinoa has absorbed all of the water, about 15 minutes, reducing heat as time goes on to maintain a gentle simmer.
- In a serving bowl, combine the chickpeas, cucumber, parsley, bell pepper, and onion. Set aside.
- In a small bowl, combine the olive oil, lemon juice, vinegar, garlic and salt.
- Once the quinoa is mostly cool, add it to the serving bowl, and drizzle the dressing on top. Toss until the mixture is thoroughly combined. Season with black pepper, to taste, and add an extra pinch of salt if necessary. For best flavor, let the salad rest for 5 minutes before serving.

Vegetable Thai Peanut

This salad recipe is made with carrots, cabbage, peas, and tossed in peanut sauce.

Ingredients

Salad

- 1 ½ cups water
- ¾ cup uncooked quinoa or millet

- 2 cups shredded purple cabbage
- 1 cup thinly sliced snow peas
- ½ cup chopped cilantro
- 1 cup grated carrot
- ¼ cup thinly sliced green onion
- Green to taste

Sauce

- 1 tablespoon honey
- 1 tablespoon rice vinegar
- ¼ cup peanut butter
- 1 teaspoon toasted sesame oil

- 3 tablespoons soy sauce
- 1 ½ tablespoons lime juice
- 1 teaspoon grated fresh ginger

Cooking

- In a medium-sized pot, combine the rinsed quinoa and 1 ½ cups water. Bring the mixture to a gentle boil over medium heat. Remove the quinoa from heat, cover the pot and let it rest for 5 minutes.
- The peanut sauce: Whisk together the peanut butter and tamari until smooth. Add the remaining ingredients and whisk until smooth.
- Combine the cooked quinoa, carrot, shredded cabbage, cilantro snow peas, and green onion. Add the peanut sauce.

Palak Paneer

Palak paneer is a very delicate and soft dish that can be described as "cream cheese dices in a thick spinach sauce".

Ingredients

- Spinach leaves - about 500 g

- Adygei cheese, 250-300 g
- 1 moderate-size onion
- 1 moderate-size tomato
- 2-3 cloves garlic
- Dry ginger – ½ teaspoon (flat)
- Chili pepper or dried pepper – to taste
- Spice mix: curry or garam masala (a blend of ground Indian spices – depends on what you like more. I prefer curry)
- Cooking butter

Preparation

- Chop spinach finely (the finer, the softer the dish will be) or shred it in a blender. (I use pre-cut and frozen spinach). Dice cheese, 1-2 cm thick. Chop the onion bulb finely. Peel the tomato and dice it finely. Mix garlic, ginger root and chili pepper in a blender/mincer/masher to obtain paste. (I used dried ginger and pepper, so I just crushed garlic in a garlic masher).

Cooking

- Fry onions in oil until light-gold. Add garlic and ginger paste and fry for two more minutes. Add tomato and stew until oil "comes out". Then add spinach and continue simmering.

- Heat up butter in the second pan, add curry and stir and fry cheese distributing all the spices evenly. Season spinach with salt, then add cheese, stir and simmer for 2-3more minutes until done.

Baked Tortilla Chips

This delicious Mexican recipe is very tasty!

Ingredients

Baked Tortilla Chips

- 16 corn tortillas
- Salt, to taste
- 2 tablespoons extra-virgin olive oil
- 2 teaspoons extra-virgin olive oil
- 3 cups 24 ounces salsa verde
- 3 tablespoons fresh cilantro, chopped

Toppings

- 3 tablespoons red onion, chopped
- 4 fried eggs
- 2 tablespoons cilantro, chopped
- 1 avocado, diced
- 1 teaspoon grated fresh ginger

Cooking

- Heat the oven to 175 degrees Celsius. Line baking sheets with parchment paper.
- Brush both sides of each tortilla with oil. Stack the tortillas, 4 at once, and slice them into 8 wedges. Repeat with remaining tortillas. Sprinkle half the salt over one pan and half over the other.
- Bake until those chips start turning golden on the edges, then remove from the oven.
- Once the chips are out of the oven, warm the olive oil in a skillet over medium heat. Add the salsa verde, being careful to avoid splatters.

- Bring the mixture to a simmer, stir in the tortilla chips and cilantro until all of the chips are lightly coated, then cover and let the mixture rest, about 5 minutes. Help yourself!

Tamantas Salad

These healthy vegetable lettuce wraps are colorful and delicious! This recipe is a perfect appetizer or light meal.

Ingredients

- Soba noodles
- 3 cups sliced purple cabbage, carrot, radish and cucumber
- ¼ cup rice vinegar
- 3 teaspoons toasted sesame oil
- 2 heads butter lettuce
- 2 tablespoons soy sauce
- 1 tablespoons sesame seeds
- Salt, to taste

Cooking

- Bring a pot of salted water to boil for the soba noodles. Remove 10 intact lettuce leaves and put off.
- In a bowl, combine the sliced vegetables, vinegar and salt, and toss to combine. Let the mixture marinate, tossing occasionally, for 15 minutes.
- Cook the soba noodles. Drain the noodles, then return them to the pot and stir in the sesame seeds, soy sauce and sesame oil. Put off.
- Top with a small handful of soba noodles, then pickled veggies. Sprinkle lightly with additional sesame seeds, and help yourself!

Boras Sauce and Pasta

Very tasty and light recipe.

Ingredients

- 1 small red onion, chopped
- 2 small potatoes
- 2 tablespoons olive oil
- 1 cup water
- 2 cloves garlic, pressed
- Salt, to taste
- ½ teaspoon onion powder
- ½ teaspoon dry mustard powder
- 7 ounces whole-grain macaroni elbows
- 1 cup raw cashews
- Apple vinegar, to taste

Cooking

- Bring a large pot of salted water to boil for the pasta. Cook according to package directions.
- Warm the oil over medium heat. Add the onion and salt and cook, about 5 minutes.
- Stir the potato, garlic, mustard powder, onion powder and salt and cook, about 2 minutes.
- Add the cashews, potatoes and water, and stir to combine. Boiled slowly, about 10 minutes.
- Pour the mixture into a blender. Add apple vinegar. Blend, about 3 minutes.
- Pour the sauce into the bowl of pasta. Stir and serve.

Halwa Pudding of Semolina

Ingredients

- 2 ¾ cups water or milk (or milk diluted with water by half)
- 1 ½ cups sugar
- 10 ribs saffron (as desired)

- ½ teaspoon grated nutmeg
- ¼ cups raisins
- ¼ cups of hazelnuts or walnuts (as desired)
- 1 cup butter
- 1½ cup semolina
- 1 teaspoon turmeric

Cooking

- Boil water (or milk), add sugar, saffron and nutmeg and boil for 1 min. Add raisins, reduce heat and let it boil. Slightly brown nuts in frying oil, crush them in a mortar and put aside. Melt butter in a pot over medium heat. Add semolina and fry it, stirring with a wooden spoon for about 10-15 minutes until it takes brown colour and oil becomes separate from the cereal. Reduce heat. Slowly pour the prepared syrup in the cereal while stirring continuously. Be careful! The mixture splashes when the syrup contacts the cereal. Stir quickly for 1 minute to crush the lumps. Add crushed nuts. Close and keep at heat for 2-3 minutes until all liquid absorbs. Mellow Halva by quick mixing several times. Serve warm or at room temperature.

Carrot Halwa

Carrot Halva is very popular in Northern India. To make a perfect Halva, it's crucial to shred carrots correctly: carrot shaving should be very thin and as long as possible. Such Halva can be cooked without milk as well. In such case add somewhat more butter and keep it heat until it gets marmalade consistency.

Ingredients

- 900 g fresh carrots
- ¾ cup butter
- 2 cups of milk
- ¾ cup of sugar
- 3 tablespoons of raisins
- 3 tablespoons of almond, sliced and slightly browned
- ½ teaspoon of ground cardamom

Cooking

- Wash carrots, peel and grate on a fine metal grater. Melt butter in a pot and add grated carrots. Fry uncovered for about 10 minutes, stirring frequently so it doesn't burn. Add milk, sugar, raisins and almond. Cook Halva for 20-30 minutes until it gets thick and turns into a homogeneous mass.
  Put halva on a serving plate. When it cools down a bit, shape it to a round sheet 2.5 cm thick. Powder ground cardamom on top. Cool down for 30 minutes, slice and serve as a dessert.

Gazpacho

Incredible cold Spanish soup.

Ingredients

2 servings:

- 2 big tomatoes
- 1 glass red water melon pulp
- 4-5 dried tomatoes
- ½ glass dry red wine
- 2 tablespoons olive oil
- ½ teaspoon salt
- 4 dried olives
- 1 red sweet pepper
- ¼ white onion
- 1 garlic clove
- 1 lemon
- ½ avocado
- 2 tablespoons sunflower stalks

Cooking

- Mix tomatoes, watermelon, dried tomatoes, pepper, onion, garlic, lemon juice oil in a blender. Season with salt, depending on the salinity of dried tomatoes.
- Slice avocado and olives.
- Ladle out soup into plates, place avocado and olives on top and add sunflower stalks.
- Dried tomatoes and olives aren't obligatory but they add a nice, pungent flavour.

Coconut Barfi

Delicious and extremely nutritive sweet, made fast without any thermal processing, just by mixing the ingredients.

Ingredients

For 20 pieces:

- 125 ml honey
- 125 ml almond, peanut or common butter
- 80 g finely chopped dates
- 80 g milk powder of medium or low fat
- 130 g grated fresh coconut slightly tamped down
- ½ tablespoon rose water

Cooking

- In a bowl mix honey and nut oil, dates and milk powder. Knead this mass with your hands until you get soft and non-sticky dough. (If necessary, add some more milk powder or water). Wash hands and wipe them dry. Roll the dough to a 50 cm long log.
- Spread grated coconut on a large sheet of wax paper, sprinkle with rose water and thoroughly mix. Divide the dough log in half or make balls out of it and roll them carefully in grated coconut.

- Place pieces in paper cases. These sweets can be stored cooled in an air-tight package up to 7 days. Warm up the sweets to room temperature before serving.

Pistachio Barfi

Yield: 24 Barfi pieces

Ingredients

- ½ glass sugar
- 1 glass water
- 3 tablespoons cooking butter or unsalted butter
- ¼ teaspoon finely powdered cardamom seeds
- ½ glass raw pistachio nuts, shelled and finely chopped
- 170 ml milk powder of medium or low fat
- 1 teaspoon of rose water or several drops of rose essence (rose oil)
- 2 drops of green food dye + 1 drop of yellow dye (optional)
- 3 tablespoons of pistachio, shelled and divided in half

Cooking

- Mix sugar with water in a 3 l low teflon-coated pan with thick bottom, and put at low heat. Stir until sugar dissolves, then increase heat and let the syrup boil quietly for 8 minutes. Remove the pan from heat and let it cool for 10 minutes. During that time, the syrup temperature will lower to 45° C. Add 1 tablespoon of cooking butter, cardamom and pistachio and add milk powder while stirring continuously. When the mixture becomes homogeneous, put the pan at medium heat and cook for 4 minutes while stirring continuously and scraping off the mass from the pan walls and bottom using a wooden spatula. After the mixture cooks down to become a thick paste, scrape off what's stuck to the pan walls and remove the pan from heat. Add the remaining 2 tablespoons of butter, rose water or rose essence and, if desired, food dye. Mix the mass until the ingredients soak completely. Scrape off the sticky mass with a rubber spatula. Spread and press down the hot mass to form a smooth rectangular sheet of 2 cm thick. When Barfi cools down completely, cut the sheet with hot knife into 24 pieces and stick a half of pistachio nut into each square piece. It's advisable to consume the cooked fudges within 4 days. Keep Barfi cooled in an air-tight package. Warm up Barfi to room temperature before serving.

Lintel Soup with Vegetables

Ingredients

- 6 cups water
- 3 teaspoons salt
- 2 cups Mung-Dala or Tur-Dala, or green shelled peas or lintel
- 675 g various vegetables: eggplant, carrots tomatoes, runner beans or pumpkin
- 50 g tamarind
- 3 tablespoons cooking butter or vegetable oil
- 1 teaspoon mustard seeds
- ½ teaspoon ground cumin seeds
- 2 teaspoons ground coriander
- ½ teaspoon Cayenne pepper or two pods of fresh hot pepper
- 1 teaspoon turmeric
- 4 tablespoons grated coconut

Cooking

- Boil salted water. Sort out, wash, dry Dal and put it in the boiling water. Boil uncovered for 10 minutes. Skim off foam, close the lid and cook at medium heat for 15-25 minutes, stirring from time to time. Dal should become soft but not cooked. In the meantime, wash and dice vegetables finely. Warm up butter in a pot and fry the mustard seeds. When seeds cease to crack, add ground spices, continue frying for a few seconds, then add vegetables (if you use eggplant, then fry it preliminary until it becomes soft). In 10 – 15 min, after all vegetables get brown, add grated coconut and fry for 2 more minutes. By that time, Dal should be ready. Add vegetables and tamarind juice. Reduce heat and cook uncovered until ready – Dal should become thick and vegetables soft.

Pie with Raisins and Spices

A wonderful treat for friends and guests. The recipe is quite simple and you only need 1 hour to get a ready to serve pie.

Ingredients

- Cottage cheese - 450 g
- Semolina - 6 tablespoons
- Sugar - 3 tablespoons
- Baking soda - 0.5 teaspoon
- Butter - 2 tablespoons
- Vanilla sugar - 1 pack
- Turmeric - 0.5 teaspoon
- Raisins - 50 g
- Sour cream - 3 tablespoons

You can also add: red chili or curry, chopped dried apricots of a raisin size.

Cooking

- Mash cottage cheese with all ingredients except sour cream and mix thoroughly. Smear the baking case with butter and powder it with semolina. Put the cottage cheese mass in the case, coat its top with sour cream and cinnamon. Bake for 30-40 minutes at 180º C. The pie can be served with fruit jam and a ball of ice cream.

Fresh Young Corn Salad

Ingredients

- Corn from 2 cobs
- Sweet peppers - I use one yellow and one small red pepper
- 1 hot pepper - one single jalapeno
- 1 teaspoon of hemp or flax oil
- 1 tablespoon of lime juice

Cooking

- The easiest way to cut off the corn from the cob is to use a thin, long fish knife with small teeth. I don't like corn oil, so I dress salad with a small quantity of hemp oil. In addition, such salad doesn't need any salt, so you may do without it.

Pears in Red Wine

Sweet and Tasty. It's a wonderful summer dessert – refreshing, fragrant and light… plus, it isn't expensive and it's easy to make. Even though it contains alcohol, everybody knows that red wine in small quantities is healthy.

Ingredients

- 1 kg of pears ripe but hard(6-7 pcs.)
- 1 lemon (peel + 1 rind)
- 1 orange (peel + 1 rind)
- 6 tablespoons of sugar (honey)
- 1 cinnamon stick
- 6 pcs. clove
- 1 pod vanilla
- Several sweet pepper peas
- Red wine

Cooking

- Use a wide pot and bring wine with lemon and apricot peels, rinds, spices and sugar (honey) to a boil. Remove from heat and close the lid. Carefully peel pears but leave the stalk. Put peeled pears to hot wine and bring to a boil at medium heat. Reduce heat to low and boil for about 20 minutes. Carefully move the pears to a bowl. Their colour will be rose thanks to wine.
- Boil down wine at small heat until it becomes light syrup. Pour the syrup over the pears through a strainer so it keeps the peels and fruit.
- Cover the pears with the upturned flat plate so they're completely immersed in syrup. Cool the dish down and place in the fridge for several hours (overnight).
- Remove the dish from the fridge 30 minutes before serving. Serve pears in dessert bowls, pour them with syrup and decorate with mint leaves or lemon Melissa leaves. The pears will draw out syrup during the night, acquire an intensive wine color and soak up with spice flavour.

Spinach and Yogurt Raita Salad

To prepare this salad any spinach species or any other green vegetables like spinach can be used. Some kinds of spinach can be grown at home in summer and autumn.

Ingredients

4 servings:

- 460 g fresh spinach
- 2 cups (475 ml) of yoghurt
- 1 teaspoon cumin seeds browned in a dry pan and ground afterwards
- 1/2 teaspoon garam masala
- 1/4 teaspoon ground black pepper
- 1 teaspoon salt

Cooking

- Cut off spinach stalks and wash leaves changing water several times. Then sink the leaves in boiling water for a minute or two, so they become soft. Drain water using a strainer, press down excess water and chop the leaves coarsely.
- Pour yoghurt in a big bowl, add spinach and other ingredients. Mix them with a fork. This salad matches well with poori. It also can be served at dinner as an additional dish.

Cucumber and Yogurt Raita Salad

According to "Ayurveda", cucumbers cool and freshen body, therefore, on a hot summer mid-day there's nothing better than a cool and aromatic cucumber Raita. To make it diverse you can always add sliced reddish, green pears, green coriander or parsley.

Ingredients

4 servings:

- ½ teaspoonful cumin seeds
- 2 middle-size cucumbers
- 1 ¼ cup (300 ml) yogurt
- ½ cup garam masala
- ½ teaspoon salt
- ¼ teaspoon ground black pepper
- 2 pinches asafoetida (if desired)

Cooking

- Brown cumin seeds in a dry pan and reduce them to powder in a mortar. Wash up cucumbers and grate them on a coarse grater. Press down excessive juice, mix it with other ingredients. Serve cooled.

Saffron Rice Pudding

Ingredients

4 servings:

- 1.5 glass of long-grain rice
- 0.5 glass of milk
- Pinch of saffron
- 6 teaspoons of butter
- 2 crushed green cardamom pods
- 2.5 cinnamon sticks
- 2 cloves
- 0.5 glasses of raisins
- 0.5 glass of sugar powder
- 0.25 glass of browned almond halves

Cooking

- Wash rice in cold water changing water several times. Then pour cold water over the rice, put at heat, bring to a boil and cook under cover for 5 minutes. Drain water. Measure out 6 teaspoons of milk in a small bowl, add saffron and let it soak for 5 minutes. Melt butter in a pan, add rice, pods of cardamom, cinnamon and cloves and fry for 2-3 minutes until the rice acquires dull color.
- Add milk, saffron milk, raisins and sugar and stir the mixture. Bring to a boil and cook at low heat under cover for 6-8 minutes until rice becomes soft and absorbs all liquid. Remove pieces of spices and serve hot after scattering almonds on the ready dish.

Paneer Sabji

This dish can be made of any vegetables and it will differ each time.

Ingredients

- ½ cabbage head
- 3-4 middle-size potatoes
- 1 tomato
- 1 red or yellow Bulgarian pepper
- 200 g of paneer (common Adygei cheese can be used)

Spices

- Cumin seeds - 1 teaspoon
- Finely sliced fresh hot red pepper (0.5 cm)
- 1 teaspoon of ginger root, finely chopped
- Curry leaves 2-3 leaves
- Ground coriander 1 teaspoon
- Pinch asafoetida
- ½ teaspoon of turmeric
- ¼ teaspoon of ground black pepper
- 1 tablespoon of methi leaves
- 3-4 tablespoons of vegetable oil or ghee (cooking butter)
- Salt, to taste

Cooking

- Take a deep heavy-bottomed frying pan and heat up cooking butter or vegetable oil, then add spices in the following sequence: cumin seeds, after the seeds begin to crack, add peeled finely cut ginger root and red pepper, after a few seconds, when the ginger root becomes brown, add coriander, black pepper, asafoetida, curry leaves and methi leaves, and, at last, turmeric. Put cottage cheese cut in about 2 cm size dices in the mixture of oil and spices, fry until golden brown on top, then add previously cut vegetables: first potato dices, then cabbage and pepper pieces. Let vegetables absorb oil and spices, and fry them at quite high heat for 2-3 minutes, while stirring carefully. Afterwards, reduce heat, add some boiling water and salt. Splash tomato with boiling water, then peel, dice and add to other vegetables. Cover the lid and simmer until done (about 20 minutes). Serve hot with rice.

Tahini — A Raw Food Recipe

This thick paste of sesame is called tahini, thini or sesame paste. Tahini sauce is added to such dishes as falafel, hummus and others, and they make sweets out of it.
The paste can be consumed with chips, cakes and flat cakes, it can be an ingredient of other, more sophisticated and complex sauces. However, we go easy and start with a small step – let's just prepare this paste.

Ingredients

- ½ cup light sesame
- ½ cup water
- Juice half lemon
- 1 clove garlic
- 1 tablespoon olive oil
- Salt, to taste

Cooking

- Grind thoroughly all ingredients until reaching cream condition. Season the mixture with a pinch of ground pepper, e.g., red pepper. Dress with vegetables, green herbs and raw hard bread. Obviously, there are may variations on tahini paste recipe – just chose the one you like best or invent your own. Eat tahini to your heart's content!

Strawberry Soup

Strawberry soup is a French dessert but not the kind of soup that we are used to eating as a starter. It's very easy to cook, and in strawberry season it's still another good way to diverse your strawberry menu.

Ingredients

2 big servings:

- Strawberry - 400-500 g
- Orange - 1 pc.
- Mint – several leaves
- Sugar - 1-3 tablespoons, depending on strawberry sweetness
- Cream or sour cream – to taste

Cooking

- Squeeze juice out of an orange. Remove leaves and stalks from strawberries, wash berries and place them in the blender bowl. It's possible to add 1-2 mint leaves, I usually do not add them though. Preferably, store strawberries in a fridge for a while to avoid a necessity to cool the strawberry soup after. In hot season, it is advisable to cool the soup before eating.
- Cover fruit with sugar and blend. Add orange juice, you will need about a half of the squeezed juice.
- Mix, taste it and add sugar, if required.
- Pour strawberry soup in a plate, decorate with mint leaves and add cream or sour cream to taste. Also, pieces of meringue or marshmallow will be suitable.
- Serve as a light, cool and refreshing dessert.

Black Bean Soup

This black bean soup recipe you make with canned beans. This soup is vegetarian and tasty.

Ingredients

- 4 cups vegetable broth
- 4 cans of black beans, rinsed
- 1 teaspoon sherry vinegar
- 2 onions, chopped
- ½ teaspoon red pepper flakes
- 4 garlic cloves, pressed
- 2 tablespoons olive oil
- 1 carrot, peeled
- Salt, to taste

Cooking

- Heat the olive oil in a pot over medium heat. Add the onions, and carrot and salt. Cook, about 15 minutes.
- Stir in the garlic and red pepper flakes and cook, about 40 seconds. Pour in the beans and broth and bring to a simmer over medium-high heat. Cook, about 35 minutes.
- Puree about 4 cups of the soup in a blender until smooth. Return the pureed soup to the pot, mixed and serve.

Baked Parmesan Zucchini

Ingredients

- 4 zucchini, quartered lengthwise
- 3 tablespoons fresh parsley leaves, chopped
- 3 tablespoons olive oil
- Salt and black pepper, to taste
- ½ cup freshly grated Parmesan
- Dried thyme, dried oregano and dried basil, to taste

Cooking

- Preheat oven to 175 degrees Celsius. In a small bowl, combine Parmesan, thyme, oregano, basil, salt and pepper, to taste.
- Place zucchini onto prepared baking sheet. Drizzle with olive oil and sprinkle with Parmesan mixture. Place into oven and bake until tender, about 15 minutes. Then broil for 2-3 minutes, or until crisp and golden brown.
- Garnished with parsley and serve.

_____
_____
_____
_____
_____
_____
_____
_____

Baked Parmesan Mushrooms

Easy, tasty mushrooms you will ever make, baked with Parmesan.

Ingredients

- 4 tablespoons olive oil
- ¼ cup grated Parmesan
- 2 tablespoons lemon juice
- 1 ½ pounds cremini mushrooms, thinly sliced
- 3 cloves garlic, minced
- Salt and black pepper, to taste

Cooking

- Preheat oven to 175 degrees Celsius. Oil a baking sheet.
- Place mushrooms in a single layer onto the prepared baking sheet. Add olive oil, lemon juice, garlic, and Parmesan; season with salt and pepper, to taste. Mixed.
- Place into oven and bake for 15 minutes, or until browned and tender, tossing occasionally. Help yourself!

_____
_____
_____
_____

Roasted Potatoes 1

These potatoes are tossed with Parmesan are delicious.

Ingredients

- 3 tablespoons olive oil
- 3 pounds red potatoes, halved
- 2 tablespoons butter

- 5 cloves garlic, minced
- 3 tablespoons chopped parsley leaves
- ¼ cup grated Parmesan
- Salt and freshly ground black pepper, to taste
- Dried oregano, dried basil, to taste

Cooking

- Preheat oven to 200 degrees Celsius. Lightly oil a baking sheet.
- Place potatoes in a single layer onto the prepared baking sheet. Add olive oil, garlic, oregano, basil and Parmesan; season with salt and pepper, to taste.
- Place into oven and bake for 35 minutes, until golden brown and crisp. Stir in butter until melted. Garnished with parsley.

Baked Green Bean

Ingredients

- 1 cup bread crumbs
- 3 eggs, beaten
- 1 ½ pounds green beans
- ½ cup flour
- Salt and freshly ground black pepper, to taste
- ½ cup grated Parmesan cheese

Cooking

- Preheat oven to 220 degrees Celsius. Lightly oil a baking sheet.
- In a large bowl, combine bread crumbs and Parmesan; season with salt and pepper, to taste, put aside.
- Dredge green beans in flour, dip into eggs, then dredge in bread crumbs mixture.
- Place green beans in a single layer onto the prepared baking sheet. Place into oven and bake for about 15 minutes.

Honey Glazed Carrots

Very tasty honey carrots!

Ingredients

- 2 tablespoons honey
- 1 tablespoons brown sugar
- 2 tablespoons butter
- 2 teaspoons chopped parsley leaves
- 16-ounce bag small Carrots
- 2 teaspoons fresh dill and
- Salt, to taste

Cooking

- Melt butter in a large skillet over medium heat. Add carrots, honey, brown sugar, dill and parsley.
- Cook, until carrots are tender, about 20 minutes.

Roasted Mushrooms

Ingredients

- 16 ounces mushrooms (to taste), thinly sliced
- 2 tablespoons butter
- ½ cup heavy cream
- 2 cloves garlic, minced
- ½ teaspoon dried oregano
- 2 tablespoons chopped fresh parsley leaves
- Salt and freshly ground black pepper, to taste

Cooking

- Melt butter in a skillet oven over medium heat. Add garlic and mushrooms, and cook, about 7 minutes.
- Stir in heavy cream and oregano; season with salt and pepper, to taste. Bring to a boil; reduce heat and simmer until slightly reduced and thickened, about 5-6 minutes.
- Garnished with parsley.

Easy Creamed Corn

Ingredients

- 6 ounces cream cheese, cubed
- 3 cups corn frozen, canned or roasted
- 2 tablespoons butter
- ½ cup milk
- 2 cloves garlic, minced
- 2 tablespoons chopped fresh parsley leaves
- 1 cup shredded cheddar cheese
- Salt and freshly ground black pepper, to taste

Cooking

- Preheat oven to 190 degrees Celsius. Oil baking dish.
- Combine cream cheese, butter and garlic in a medium saucepan over medium high heat. Stir in milk until smooth, about 4 minutes. Stir in corn until well combined, about 3minutes.
- Spread corn mixture into the prepared baking dish; sprinkle with cheese. Bake about 20 minutes.

Healthy Salad

Wonderful Healthy Salad is perfect.

Ingredients

- 1 apple, shredded
- ½ cup grated Parmesan cheese
- 2 tablespoons olive oil
- 1 cup shredded green cabbage
- 1 cup shredded red cabbage
- 1 cup shredded carrot
- 1 tablespoon apple cider vinegar
- Salt and freshly ground black pepper, to taste
- 2 tablespoons chopped fresh parsley leaves
- 1 tomato, shredded

Cooking

- In a large bowl, combine the green cabbage, red cabbage, carrot, apple and tomato.

- Whisk together the Parmesan cheese, olive oil, vinegar, parsley leaves, salt and pepper, to taste.
- Pour mixture over cabbage mixture and stir. Help yourself!

Garlic Roasted Broccoli

Perfect and easiest garlic roasted broccoli.

Ingredients

- 24 ounces broccoli
- 4 tablespoons olive oil
- 2 cloves garlic, minced
- ½ cup freshly grated Parmesan
- Salt and freshly ground black pepper, to taste
- Juice of 1 lemon
- 2 tablespoons chopped fresh parsley leaves
- 100 g mushrooms, to taste

Cooking

- Preheat oven to 220 degrees Celsius. Oil a baking sheet.

- Place broccoli florets in a single layer onto the prepared baking sheet. Add olive oil, mushrooms and garlic; season with salt and pepper, to taste.
- Place into oven and bake for about 10 minutes.
- Sprinkled with Parmesan, lemon juice and chopped fresh parsley leaves.

Baked Asparagus with Sauce

This is a simple and delicious recipe.

Ingredients

- 1 teaspoon apple vinegar
- 1 bunch fresh asparagus, trimmed
- 2 tablespoons olive oil
- 1 tablespoon soy sauce
- 2 tablespoons butter
- 1 red pepper
- 1 carrot
- 1 small beetroot
- Salt, to taste

Cooking

- Preheat oven to 200 degrees Celsius.
- Arrange the asparagus on a baking sheet. Coat with olive oil, cut and add red pepper, beetroot and carrot with salt. Bake, about 25 minutes.

- Melt the butter in a saucepan over medium heat. Stir in soy sauce and apple vinegar. Pour over the baked asparagus to serve.

Roasted Potatoes 2

This recipe is perfect, light and tasty.

Ingredients

- 1 pound red potatoes, diced
- 1 yellow onion
- 1 tablespoon butter
- 1 tablespoon honey
- 1 tablespoon olive oil
- 1 carrot, diced
- Salt and ground black pepper, to taste

- Preheat oven to 175 degrees Celsius.
- Place potatoes and top with onion and carrot. In a bowl, mix melted butter, honey, olive oil, salt and pepper. Add to potatoes.
- Bake in the oven preheated 175 degrees Celsius, about 35 minutes.

Made in the USA
Las Vegas, NV
01 October 2023